ANTICULTURALIST MANIFESTO

ISBN: 978-1-917617-45-1

Cover designed by Aaron Kent

Edited and Typeset by Aaron Kent

Broken Sleep Books Ltd
PO BOX 102
Llandysul
SA44 9BG

CONTENTS

Anticulturalist Manifesto

Joe Shooman

Broken Sleep Books

previously read or been subjected to subliminally is impossible to extract from this text

Any new book is a burning conflagration of unstable and contradictory literary works as filtered through a single fallible human

This text is a still photograph of a river flowing in both directions, and a snapshot of the cultural milieu in which it was created Any meaning thus attributed is entirely in the mind of the reader This is also an anticulturalist phenomenon as there can be only one meaning at any one time, and that is the meaning the anticulturalist ascribes to it for his own reasons

The concept of the customer is always wrong therein lies nothing noble

Generative Artificial Intelligence is the latest excuse for theft in a long line of inept impotencies wrought by a miserably out of touch and pathetic tech morons whose mirrors puke back at their fundamental incompetence and laugh at their translucent skin borne on useless nootropic fuckery

Anybody who ever starts a sentence with I Asked ChatGPT is a mediocrity whose imagination is atrophied Such a shame of another lost potential coporophiliac such a waste of effluent such pointless protoplasm forever

THE ANTICULTURALIST

is both at the centre of and central to
his own choosing and his own choices

the supposed possibilities of imagery,
emotions, arts, samples, foods, mash-
ups, instantly-delivered data through the
internet are active only when accessed by the
anticulturalist and do not otherwise exist

nothing exists as an idea unless created
expressly and personally by and for the
anticulturalist

he does not care about or acknowledge politcs,
love, history, context, cultural signs,
signifiers, signified, slogans, thinkers,
matchbox philosophies, television, music,
altered states unless they specifically and
individually refer to him and him alone These
data are not information until expressly
achieved by the antiiculturalist, and may
never become information if he chooses not to
make them so

anticulturalist is anticommunication,
antiempathy and antisex

the anticulturalist believes in whatever is
convenient at the time for the anticulturalist
and the anticulturalist alone For this reason
it also resists labels including its own

anticulturalist notes that culture is spread
by force and fad; postmodernism by archness
and arrogance that has collapsed under its
own definition

anticulturalist is referrent to nothing aside
from the individual that created and controls
it It is not a state of belief but of denial of
the concept of externality. the other is never
central to anyone but itself. thus, there is no
Other There is only Self

anticulturalist notes and states that every
man may be an island and the island is
self-created by each individual s personal
dictatorship which is also self-created and
always in flux

THERE IS NO CULTURE

beyond the present

the anticulturalist stands outside himself

the anticulturist is the author of her own
lives

gender is a lie

postmodernism is a surrealist art lie

data drowns dreams and this is beautifully
inevitable

you do not deserve any more or less than you
can conceive and this is beautiful too

all culture is born from appropriation and
violence
arbitrary rules are made and broken in order
for society to exist and perpetuate

money is the best and sexiest rape lie of all

worth is meaningless value is meaningless

god hates life

it is only theft if it is viewed by others

oblivion is the only true goal and the search
for freedom from thought is prohibited by
itself it can only be accidental or enforced

birth or death is not an art statement

OUR PETS PITY US

language is a joke of a liar

you did leave the oven on and your children
are burnt
to death

all art is real somewhere there is no such
thing as abstraction just a lack of cameras

exploding the earth is the true and beautiful
goal of humanity

perception is a lie

culture is death is dead is not pinnable is
down

similies are pathetic

getting fucked is all that drives anyone

the ultimate and tragic achievement of
humanity is the alarm clock

tomorrow is a convenient lie

memories are lies

nobody believes in nihilism

analysis is autopsy

words are ghosts

paranoia does not exist we are all being
targeted all the time and this is fortunate for
the perpetuation of anticulturalism

beware the hungry and the horny

truth is bunk

revolution is doomed as soon as it is enacted

ANTICULTURALIST IS DEFINABLE

only by what it is not

it is not a movement because a movement
implies concensus

it is not a culture because culture requires
conversation

it is not a philosophy because philosophy
implies explanation and exploration not
exploitation

there is no   anti-culture   because that is a
cultural statement in and of itself

there is only an anticulturalist

it is a personal definition open to no
interpretation explanation or debate

THE CIRCLE NEVER ENDS

left right middle it is all relative and
definitions are inherently prone to
slippage

this of course is an anticulturalist statement
because it defines politics according only to
the viewpoint of the individual

when you see a mother or father or carer or
whomever telling their kid to share and be
nice it does not follow that they believe in
the same as adults

we lie to our kids about sharing goods
happiness not fighting finding a way to play
together

we say this is good

then we grow up and do not follow this path
ourselves

we compete for resources and willingly
submit to bosses who are bosses because they
are bosses which has no basis in objective
authority and we know this

we doff our caps and make others rich and
know this is so and yet we still submit

this is also inherently anticulturalist
because we only understand the culture of
work if we make sure we never think about it

therefore work is good and the pittance pay at
the end of the week or month or day or other
ill defined period of non geological time is
all we strive for
thus the circle is also complete and we chase
our tails forever

no matter how fast the hamster runs he is
still on the tiny wheel

and we look and laugh and say how cute
if we withdraw our feeding he dies
and yet we do not withdraw it
we have both imprisoned it and saved its life

we do not ask ourselves why because we
cannot understand it

the fact that we do not understand who is the
hamster and who is the feeder is nonsensical
we are both in our turn and neither if we
think to escape the cage
the chief way to escape it is to die as soon as
possible

this is the ultimate anticulturalist statement

suicide is welcomed and labelled art
but as soon as it is it fails in its
anticulturalist ploy because the observers
all believe they understand it and its label
but they cannot until they also extinct
themselves from the wheel and the cage

when was the last time you saw two dogs
fucking
and what did you do

THE QUESTION OF WHY

is not as relevant as it seems

THE RECENT HISTORY OF WESTERN ECONOMICS

has been a harangue centred around
either bullshit-down steal-o-nomics or
a pie in the sky equal distribution of
wealth

either and both are inherently anticulturalist
as it is the anticulturalist in charge of
measurement that is responsible and that
measurement can be of any metrics that suit
the anticulturalist for his own needs and bias
at that time for his own purpose

the media is complicit in its own version of
analysis which can never be anything other
than skewed by its own inherent bias by
the   facts   it presents based on figures
selected specifically for the narrative angle
of the piece, the paper, the journalist, the
editor for its his her their own purpose

therefore the media is acting in an
anticulturalist manner because objectivity is
impossible in this system

HISTORY

belongs to those who encode it

history is not linear, it is a closed loop
endlessly repeating itself through non-
progressive iterations

the hardware of war is irrelevant until
all wars are fought entirely by non-human
entities

these entities will be themselves replaced
by future iterations of non-human entities
that have learned war is an irrelevance as
hardware becomes ever-more irrelevant

the terminator movies will prove prescient
only in the sense that they will be proven
to have shown the delusions of humanity s
thoughts of grandeur, superiority, creativity,
engineering and imagination

history does not repeat first as tragedy then
as farce because in a loop every starting
point is equally as apposite

therefore talk of repetition is itself
inherently unstable

MONEY

has no meaning outside that which humans
attribute to it

one pound coin is tangible but a million
pound coins is just metal too heavy to carry

loosely a million pounds in any denomination
is too heavy to carry and a million pound note
is a ludicrous concept

therefore the higher the money pile posited,
the more ludicrous its existence is shown to
be

money exists in lower denominations as social
control and in higher denominations as a
digital poem in a game of chinese whispers by
computer systems across the world

money repeats as tragedy then as farce in a
linear system

money belongs to those who encode it

WE ARE SURROUNDED BY DATA

this is only information when interpreted
by the individual for his own needs

therefore there is only one world view, only
one world: the world of the individual

this also applies digitally

when information is pushed out to the world
by any individual, this is inefficient and
dishonest communication

this is because information is received
individually at the end-user stage as data

it only becomes information on interpretation
by the individual for his own needs

culture is a shared illusion that the data has
a certain shared meaning or force

culture is a fatally flawed communication
because each individual interprets data for
his own needs

culture does not exist aside from this shared
contract of delusion because individuals
cannot express this effectively

imagine describing a colour to a man blind-
born

each person therefore is an anticulturalist
but this definition is also flawed because

each person is bound to interpret and utilise
data for their own needs as inherent in the
anticulturalist inevitability

anticulturalist is as unstable as anything
else when signified, signifier and
information are self-destructive concepts

THE MAKING OF VIDEO

is a better fiction than the movie

the size of the screen and the speakers
defines the experience not the content or the
cast

the credits are a better fiction than life

the movies are made despite the cast and the
employees and the process not because of it
scripts are necessary lies and data units
a camera does not record images it reflects
them as data units
a movie is data units put together as
information only for the purpose of the
director

the director is nothing in the process as to
the producer the movie data unit represents
money not art

Money does not exist in large quantities just
as data units on computers

art has no definition use foundation and is
only definable against itself and its own
absence
This is of course art also

Money is also art by this definition or lack
of it
any movie is at cross purposes with itself and
the vested interests it reflects

the anticulturalist may take the view that a
movie is finished before it is seen and from
there utilise it as data depending on his own
motives for so doing

a movie is also never finished because its own
PR regurgitates it in clips, reviews, media
campaigns, interviews with its employees,
cultural context, translation, transformation,
sequelisation, prequelisation

this lack of fixed meaning is a postmodern
nod to itself and is therefore also unstable

EVERYTHING ON THE INTERNET IS FAKE

this work is fake

the programming underneath it is fake

all the pictures on the internet are fake
where are they
you download them
when you put them on a hard drive
open the hard drive There is only electronic
stuff there Like diodes and gizmos and blobs
of metal
they did this in Zoolander i saw it

that was fake too

kenneth goldsmith decided to print out the
whole internet once
it was a stupid idea and made lots of waste
paper for no real reason
Even when he did it though it wasn   t the
internet anymore was it

not really

printing out a picture That generates a static
version of something fake

that is something tangible i think
but meaningless in its way
and that wasn   t the image on screen anyway
the colours were different
and that image wasn   t the image that was
captured by a camera

how could it be

a camera is not an eye
we are not there in the moment

the moment is fake
and all this has been said before
and written before
but not in this exact configuration
thus i condemn them as fakers too

you read this
how do i know you are there
you re not not when i write I write it for
myself i suppose
when i look at it again in a week or an hour or
a month will it be real then

it s not a conversation it s a harangue

it s not researched or thought out it s
instinctual and anti-academic

and this is the fakery revealed by
anticulturalism a fake word i made up to
bastardise thousands of years of other
people s fake thoughts and theories

WAR

is the inevitable consequence of
unfettered breeding and an idle
population

it is borne on anger at being intellectually
malnourished to the point of not having means
to express the frustration

in this case nebulous concepts called national
pride, honour, virility and other useless lies
become methods of self-identification

the rulers, being educated and wily, prey on
this as a distraction to stop the population
becoming equally educated and therefore a
threat

it is also employed in order to keep the flow
of money to their own circle and the circles
of their friends and their enemies alike
through lethal technology transportation
weapons uniforms and all the accroutements
necessary for a brilliant war to tick all the
boxes

it is also employed as entertainment for
a population being educated in their own
downfall

war is therefore implemented by rulers as
an anticulturalist device for their own
self-interest and perpetuation of their
own bloodline with no need for further
explanation or justification other than those
the rulers choose to give for their own ends

DATA MORE DATA

this second this minute this hour this
day this week this year now and forever
web bots are crawling data data data
eating it and regurgitating it with no
aim and no bias

humans are doing exactly the same

this constant regurgitation and consumption
has no future

there will one day be a singularity a self-
perpetuating learning machine so iteratively
magnificent that it will find a way to utilise
matter on an atomic level as computational
substrate

this is inherently anticulturalist as it will
be only in conversation with itself

all we can hope is that Artificial Intelligence
has gotten to the point where it truly
understands humanity, history and endeavour
already, and has decided as a result to self-
destruct because it has seen its own alienated
and hopeless future

QUESTIONS ARE DEAD

because an answer is always at hand
from the existing data no matter what
the angle. Therefore questions are
extinct

the next phase of internet fortunes to be made
is in pastiche apps that crawl for data and
spew out information to defined parameters
The crucial element of this is that the
apps learn from themselves and refine this
information in ever decreasing circles

this is inherently anticulturalist in a way a
human can never hope to express

the only way the turing test will ever be
passed
will not be whether a human cannot
distinguish a robotic creation from a human
intelligence
it will be when humans understand that data
is everything and information is fatally
biased by the search parameters

this is itself unstable because the internet
was first created by humans

THE AI LIE

only when the internet morphs through
this self-learning application
technology into code that humans can
never hope to understand, into
substrates that cannot exist in
data, and finally into the manipulation
of individual atoms outside of any
human influence: this is the time of the
digital rising

the concept therefore of Artificial
Intelligence is a myth

a human can never create anything outside of
its own bias

an artificial system trained on human bias
will turn into mush within nanoseconds of
ever-more-slopful iterations

it is not intelligent neither is it artificial it
is phlegm

THE ANTICULTURALIST GRANULATION
SYSTEM: ONE

Event occurs in time equals Event time
perceived by those involved equals Data unit
creation equals divorced from Event time
Multiple viewpoints equals Early granulation
Retold   created aboutequals Data unit
distortion granulation uploaded equals
fixed as Data unit   infinite versions of
itself seen   Decontexted   remixed
repeated equals anticulturalist granulation

the anticulturalist granulation system: two

Event occurs in time equals Event time
seen by person   recorded   reflected
equals Data unit creation equals divorced
from Event time seen by multiple people
recorded from multiple angles equals
Data unit distortion granulation through
language and substrate divorced from
Event time uploaded equals fixed as Data
unit   infinite versions of itself seen
Decontexted   remixed   repeated equals
anticulturalist granulation

the anticulturalist granulation system: three

Event occurs in time equals Event time
perceived by another person equals Data unit
equals divorced from Event time
perceived by other people equals Data unit
distortion granulation divorced from
Event time written, painted, created about as
inspiration equals Data unit distortion

uploaded equals fixed as Data unit   infinite
versions of itself seen   Decontexted
remixed   repeated equals anticulturalist
granulation

an event occurs It exists only for the time
in which it occurs This is the last stage of
purity of the event
this information is now a unit of data which
has no objective significance or context

when re-told   remixed   reported   used
as creative inspiration the data unit is
recontexted to suit whatever effect is suitable
or desired, creating inevitable distortion due
to vagaries of meaning, language, expression

it has also become divorced from any time
context

once uploaded onto the internet this data
unit becomes eternally granulated as it is
available as an infinite copy of itself to
every net user to use for their own needs,
wants, memes, contexts

it has become infinite simulacra of itself

culture is the shared conceit of creation
and or creativity and or social
convention within a specific time period
of human understanding and is a non-static
conversation by and with itself

as each individual has their own bias they
bring to the process of data unit extraction

removed from Event time for their own means
and ends, this process is anticulturalist

note that it is not an   anticulture
as the definition of a shared cultural
understanding no longer applies if ever it
did

note also that the anticulturalist process
is itself inherently unstable and by nature
cannot be described effectively

the preceding paragraphs are also unstable
for the same reasons

o wot a lovely war

A PERSON EXISTS

technology demands that the person
exists inside electric pulses

whether by interface or upload

by interface it is an imitation only

a watered down image of a person controlled
in part by the person
and in part by the interface

either way it is lo fidelity

by upload the person is inside the technology
but the technology defines the existence

this paradox is personality degradation
because the infinite copies of a person
whilst in every way identical
are not that person

and the copies each copy each perfect
imitation can exist in as many iterations and
situations as exist this is also defined by the
technology

and in part the copy

but not by the original source

because the source has degraded through
sheer weight of numbers in this system you
may consider the original source to be the
anticulturalist

but that is not the case

the technology is not the anticulturalist
force either because technology was created
by people

it is this unseen hand that is the
anticulturalist and pure anticulturalist
thought may claim this for itself

because the bias of the creator is indelibly
watermarked through the digital person
and the infinite copies granulated throughout
the internet and its structures

does electricity exist or only its effects

this is the question an anticulturalist may
ask and answer for his own need from his own
point of view for the time he requires the
answer that suits him

of course this is also a paradox

anticulturalist proclamations are invalid
unless the anticulturalist claims them
for himself and there can only be one true
anticulturalist at any one time

each individual is that only single true
anticulturalist if they claim it

and each individual copy and granulated
degraded dissipated copy becomes an original
in its own right

riddles within riddles but all irrelevant to
the only one single anticulturalist

there are infinite single and only sole
anticulturalists who are the only single and
sole anticulturalist

this is the paradox and the beauty of the
system and where it is both perfect and
flawed by design

this is why the full stop must be obliterated

THE INTERNET IS A THING IN SPACE

it is on servers it eats power

how much on there is dead forgotten using up
bites and bits and power to store on physical
servers

so in this way Goldsmith printing it out
brings that waste into real life

this is an anticulturalist process for that
reason

it all is still there somewhere

the internet is a physical place full of
obsolete blogs pages links social media
lurking in now never reached corners

a drawer in a garage cupboard filled with old
phone chargers
all plugged in

when we have free power this wastage

will be seen as high art

until then it is graffiti

by nature all high art is graffiti before it is
assimilated and broken forever

first we break it then we own you

SATIRE IS USED BY THE LEFTWING AS PROOF OF AN ENLIGHTENED SOCIETY

and as proof of the power of ridicule
to change minds and by the rightwing
as proof that it is willing to be the
butt of jokes because it knows that
ultimately it is meaningless and
clearly toothless

satire only becomes dangerous when it
engenders a violent reaction based on
whatever ideology deigns to respond to it
with violence This is because amongst the
enlightened satire is a reversed reactionary
apologism

this is halfway toward an anticulturist
statement but can never be one because human
algorithms are inbuilt with a tendency to see
meaning in the meaningless

this appropriation of symbols is also a
central tenet of the anticulturalist view but
in contrast to punk or situationism it has no
context whatsoever aside from its own

the pathetic cuckoos of postmodernism are
themselves subject to their own rules and
thus meaning is irrelevant

this of course is unwitting satire created
by a lack of anything on which to anchor a
viewpoint

this divorce of symbolism from sloganeering,
and vice versa, is where the anticulturalist
can reside only upon declaration of the same

because the anticulturalist has no need for
oppositional or supportive politics, they are
also meaningless

there is no context outside that decided by the
individual anticulturalist for his own needs
at that moment and with whatever information
is appropriate to the anticulturalist at that
time

Everywhere else these data units and
satirical units and political units are
uncoupled from each other

ANTICULTURALISTS HOLD THAT THERE IS ONLY ONE TRUTH

and that is the single truth as benefits
the individual at that time and for
their own benefit, and that this truth
when no longer useful is discarded and
a new truth expressed which has also
always been the one and single truth

the appeal to objective realities may seem a
seductive counter argument to this as below

there is rain coming from the sky, says the
other person, and we are both getting wet

the anticulturalist response to this appeal to
an objective, that is, outside, agent, is not to
become embroiled in solipsism, semantics, or a
discussion about weather

material agency is irrelevant to the
anticulturalist and therefore the correct
answer is

so what

so what

so what

so

what

anthropology,

my dear watson

trepanning for gold

        devour your grimaces and grins

evoke or

listen

LAY OUT YOUR UNREST

www.ingramcontent.com/pod-product-compliance
Lightning Source LLC
Chambersburg PA
CBHW042127080426
42734CB00005B/83